SANCTUARY

SANCTUARY

Creative Homes
with Intention,
Meaning & Beauty

BY IN BED

Hardie Grant

BOOKS

LUIGI GHIRRI PUGLIA

ISAMU NOGUCHI RETROSPECTIVE 1992

JB BLUNK

FRANÇOIS HALARD   SAUL LEITER

Contents

Introduction

We are deeply inspired by the homes of creatives. Homes that feel authentic and truly unique to those who live in them. Not trend-driven or overly designed, but rather havens that have been curated with pieces collected over a lifetime, handed down, discovered on travels or while rummaging through antique stores and markets, and brought together with innate style. Homes that feel genuine and warm – an extension of their inhabitants.

This is the inspiration behind our textiles brand, IN BED, and through this medium we have featured countless creatives at home in our journal. The people we feature in the *IN BED Journal* are rarely selected just because of their home. There's as much focus on who they are and how they choose to live and create a life.

This book features homes from all over the globe, from a share house in Collingwood to a rural retreat in Devon and a treetop abode in Mexico City. These stories offer much to learn about the universal truths of creating a home and sanctuary wherever you are in the world.

First, it's not effortless; it takes time and intention. Slowly building a collection and a home over a long period and finding the right pieces, which hold meaning as well as beauty. It's always a work in progress.

Second, showing love and care to your home is an act of self-love and love for those with whom you share a home. Creating a sanctuary in which you want to spend your time can ease the stress of a hard day, bring family closer together and foster creative connection.

We hope you find the same inspiration and joy in these homes that we have over the years.

Pip Vassett
Founder, IN BED

TILLY
BARBER

Eltham, Australia

Just forty minutes from Melbourne's CBD resides Tilly Barber, founder of furniture design studio Monde and the sustainably led styling service Homebody. Tilly's incredible home is a large studio situated on a family compound that was built by the prolific Australian architect Alistair Knox. Embracing this unconventional space, Tilly has created a home filled with unique objects, a place where she and her six-year-old son, Marley, can live simply and close to nature.

'Living in the studio is like living in a private bush pavilion,' Tilly explains. 'Although it isn't large, the facade is made entirely of glass doors that open up to five acres of native bushland. This gives the space a sense of openness, and within it I've been able to create zones for entertaining, work, play, bathing and sleep.'

Discussing her bedroom, Tilly reflects on the initial challenges of furnishing an open-plan home. 'My first instinct was to install custom shoji panels to create division between the sleeping and living spaces. Although I might come back to this idea, I have grown to be quite fond of how the bedroom and living spaces exist as one. Somehow, it is spacious, harmonious and calm. In bed, I can see trees from every angle, directly outside or above through the skylight. In the afternoon, long shadows and warm light fill that area of the house. It's a really nice space for stretching, reading or taking a nap with the doors open.'

Art and objects of distinction hold great significance in Tilly's home, each with its own unique provenance. 'Accumulating artwork is such a nice, slow process,' she says. 'I only have a handful of pieces, but they all hold a special story, memory or meaning.' Tilly takes pride in the unique collection of art adorning her walls, with special pieces by artists including Camille Moir, Anna Feidler and

Allie Webb. This varied group of works, from weavings to linocut prints, is staggered throughout the home, introducing pops of colour to the existing earthy palette.

Reflecting on the philosophy behind Monde, Tilly shares its origins as an exploration of design and manufacturing. 'It started with a design for a foam chair with removable and interchangeable upholstery. My vision for Monde was to make furniture that is ultra-functional, highly durable and environmentally conscious. We researched and explored various recycling possibilities and processes, as well as recyclable mediums, to ensure a minimal environmental footprint.'

Tilly's commitment to sustainability is evident in her home. 'Most of the other things we own are handmade or found items from kerbside collection, Marketplace and op shops,' she says. 'I'm constantly sourcing and acquiring furniture for Homebody and this has meant some amazing pieces have passed through our home – but a notable piece that I've held on to is our coffee table. Though it looks simple and unassuming, it was purpose-built in the sixties to store Knox's architectural plans. The table lifts open to reveal a storage compartment underneath. It came with the house and recently I had the honour of restoring it back to its original condition after it had been painted with awful mission brown.'

Throughout Tilly's studio, we bear witness to the harmonious blend of nature, art and thoughtful design. It's a space that embodies the young creative's values and showcases her dedication to a home that is at once beautiful, functional and warm.

'Living in the studio is like living in a private bush pavilion. Although it isn't large, the facade is made entirely of glass doors that open up to five acres of native bushland. This gives the space a sense of openness, and within it I've been able to create zones for entertaining, work, play, bathing and sleep.'

Eltham, Australia

13

Tilly Barber

16   Tilly Barber

Eltham, Australia

'Accumulating artwork is
such a nice, slow process.
I only have a handful
of pieces, but they all hold
a special story, memory
or meaning.'

Tilly Barber

ANNIE NGUYEN

Koreatown,
United States

Filled with an array of books and art, Annie Nguyen's beautifully curated Koreatown apartment is a haven of calm and an escape from the bustle of big-city living.

'I live in an apartment and was so excited about moving into this place because of the ample light and space,' Annie says. Having spent years in a much smaller space, she found the transition to a roomier apartment a much-welcome change. 'My favourite aspect of this apartment is the warm lighting all year round. Around sunset, the living room turns into a warm yellow-orange. It is my absolute favourite time of day.'

In Annie's realm, simplicity reigns supreme. Her bedroom embodies this ethos, meticulously designed to be a sanctuary for rest and relaxation. Emphasising the importance of maintaining a calm environment, Annie has intentionally kept the room free from electronics. Neutral colours, such as off-whites, light greys and beiges, are tastefully combined with an ash-coloured wood and white palette, further contributing to the overall sense of tranquillity.

Within the confines of her home, Annie surrounds herself with objects of meaning, including cards and photographs from loved ones and an ever-growing Noguchi lamp collection. 'Their shapes always inspire me, and having them on just makes me feel so calm.'

Annie's passion for design sprouted at a young age, sparked by her fascination with coding and designing web pages at the tender age of twelve. This early interest eventually led her to pursue graphic design in college, where she shaped her creative skills and found her true calling. At twenty-four, Annie ventured to Los Angeles, driven by a desire to carve a path in the world of design. 'I'm so grateful for having design principles as a foundation because I think it really allowed me to apply it to various areas of the creative industry. I've been fortunate to have opportunities in music, fashion, experiential, 3D and live action. The way I view it is, no matter the medium, the same rules of composition and storytelling still apply.'

When asked about projects close to her heart, Annie shifts her focus to the experiences she has enjoyed. 'When I reflect on the projects I've done, it's not so much the end product that is special to me, but the experience I had while doing the project,' she explains. 'I think that what I do, being primarily in marketing, is so ephemeral. But those memories I made with the people I worked with are what stay with me. It is imperative to me that we have fun doing the work and that people are treated with kindness and respect.'

Annie's creative process is guided by a macro perspective, and she starts off viewing her projects with a bird's-eye view. 'I always start at thirty thousand feet. It's important for me to figure out the overall story of what it is I want to say,' she explains. The visual elements, mediums and project stages fall into place, each contributing to the narrative. 'I'm a very process-driven and systematic thinker,' she adds, highlighting the importance of a structured approach even in the midst of exploring aesthetics.

Annie enjoys her home's proximity to an abundance of good food and culture; however, her heart remains firmly tethered to her hometown. 'I was born and raised in Honolulu and try to go back at least once a year,' she says. 'My family and closest friends all live in Honolulu and, in that respect, I still consider it home to me.'

Koreatown, United States

Annie Nguyen

'My favourite aspect of this apartment is the warm lighting all year round. Around sunset, the living room turns into a warm yellow-orange. It is my absolute favourite time of day.'

Annie Nguyen

Koreatown, United States

Annie Nguyen

MAGGIE
DYLAN

& JULIAN
KELLY

Coorabell, Australia

From their home for all seasons in the Byron hinterland, Maggie Dylan and Julian Kelly have had a profound impact on Byron Bay's cafe culture.

'We have lived in a beautiful barn in Coorabell for about four years, which we found by chance in the local paper,' Maggie explains. 'It's been a special place for us, and its walls are filled with many memories. We cook here, play music here, read and riff on all things art, business, love and life. We feel very lucky to be here. Our landlords are amazing, and the property is a bit of a mix of wild beauty and considered design. We live together with Cohen, our dog, and his cat brother, Len.'

Their space embraces the duo's artistic nature and provides a backdrop for gardening, cooking and reading together. 'We like to keep the home itself pretty loose. I have the attention span of a goldfish and we can both be quite messy, so our home space needs to accommodate that. It is our office/bedroom/art studio/kitchen. It has housed us lovingly. It housed us as our businesses grew and we needed that sanctuary. It housed my dad in some of the final moments of his life while we cared for him. It has housed us in love and in grief.'

The home also shows the couple's sentimental side, evident in their most cherished objects. 'Our plants are very special, most of which we adopted when they were so young back in our previous Melbourne life,' says Maggie. 'Everything in our home is pretty special to us. We don't like to bring anything into our space unless we already have a purpose or place for it. There is no storage, so everything is "on display", so to speak. Our books and music collection are precious to us as they are sentimental and provide us with the connection to the outside world - living in the hills of Byron is very isolating!'

Among their favourite pieces is an old Japanese door used as a bedhead, complete with carpenter's notes, and macramé pieces crafted by Maggie's dad during a long hospital stay in the 1970s. Greenery is in no short supply, with potted plants of all shapes and sizes punctuating empty spaces throughout the home.

Looking back on the inception of their much-loved cafe, Maggie recalls, 'We started Folk in what was maybe the rough area of Byron at the time. We took on the lease without having visited the building. On the first day of renovations, we took the big grated security bars off the windows and cut a giant hole in the frontage for our front door. Our neighbours were aghast - were we crazy, everything will get stolen, this isn't going to work in this area, et cetera. When they discovered we would only be serving vegetarian food, their jaws dropped even further. But we felt like it was the best area for it.'

Maggie and Julian envisaged an inclusive space for the locals - a little community garden reflecting the values of the area.

'Byron has had massive growth since that time, and sometimes it feels as though Folk has come to represent an aspect of Byron in itself,' Maggie says. 'When we first started, we were just a bunch of gritty kids and old hippies, lounging on the lawn, sipping coffees, and sharing what was really restaurant-quality food from an old shack out the front of a caravan park.'

Much like the couple's businesses, Maggie and Julian's home stands as a reflection of their creativity, sentimentality and commitment to cultivating spaces that embody warmth and a true sense of retreat.

'Everything in our home is pretty special to us. We don't like to bring anything into our space unless we already have a purpose or place for it. There is no storage, so everything is "on display", so to speak.'

Maggie Dylan & Julian Kelly

Maggie Dylan & Julian Kelly

Maggie Dylan & Julian Kelly

'We like to keep the home itself pretty loose. I have the attention span of a goldfish and we can both be quite messy, so our home space needs to accommodate that.'

Coorabell, Australia

39

Maggie Dylan & Julian Kelly

JOHN &
JULI BAKER

West Toronto,
Canada

It's in West Toronto that John and Juli Baker live with their two children, Howell and Elodie, in a home tucked on top of their store, Mjölk, a merged lifestyle shop and gallery that celebrates functionality and craftsmanship in equal measure. The store takes its cue from the duo's passion for Japanese and Scandinavian design, an aesthetic mirrored upstairs in their family home.

It wasn't design but music (and serendipity) that united John and Juli initially – they met at a small bar in Toronto. Recounts John, 'Our timing wasn't ideal as Juli was about to embark on a trip to Iceland, and I was still living an hour outside of the city. However, through friends, we found each other once Juli was back from her trip, and we had an immediate connection and we jumped into the relationship.'

The apartment has been home for well over a decade, but a renovation in 2013 truly transformed it. 'The space was inspired by a mix of Japanese and Scandinavian living, the upstairs being white with pale floors and lots of sunlight, while the second-floor living spaces have warm beige lime plaster walls, shoji screens and a warmer Japanese ryokan feel. We worked with our long-time collaborators Studio Junction on the interior of the space, and they were the ones who executed all of the beautiful millwork.'

Among the much-loved pieces in the creative couple's home is a George Nakashima conoid bench, made by his daughter, Mira. John and Juli's enduring connection with the Nakashima family has been one of significant meaning. 'We hosted the first Nakashima exhibition in Canada, and this was one of the main pieces in the show,' says John. 'We drove down to New Hope when our daughter was only four months old to meet Mira and interview her for our Mjölk book. We really got swept up in their work; it's some of the most beautiful furniture ever made.

With our bench, we were able to select the wood for the slab seat, and working with them was such a meaningful experience.'

John and Juli's mornings at home are dedicated to spending time as a family and, of course, good coffee. 'Usually Howell sneaks into our bed at some point in the night, and then wakes us up at least thirty minutes before our alarm rings. He will ask me to get up and come upstairs to the kitchen with him. Sometimes I'll spring up, and sometimes I'll protest a little. Eventually, we come to the kitchen where I'll immediately fill the kettle and turn on the burner, and Howell will grind the coffee for us and put it in our French press. Usually at this time, Elodie is already up and fully dressed and ready for the day, and she and Juli will come up together once the smell of coffee wafts downstairs. While we drink coffee, it's all about getting the kids fed and ready for school. I'll walk them to school while Juli does a bit of yoga and gets ready.'

The domestic hasn't seen the duo forsake their focus on good design, but the home continues to be a source of inspiration. Having now celebrated ten years in business, John and Juli reflect on their journey with a sense of gratitude and a clear understanding that their design sensibilities and considered way of living will continue to inform the business. 'We always look to our own daily life when making decisions to add items to the store. We need to be able to envision using these pieces, and really wanting them to be in our lives.'

West Toronto, Canada

John & Juli Baker

48 John & Juli Baker

West Toronto, Canada

John & Juli Baker

'The space was inspired by a mix of Japanese and Scandinavian living, the upstairs being white with pale floors and lots of sunlight, while the second-floor living spaces have warm beige lime plaster walls, shoji screens and a warmer Japanese ryokan feel.'

John & Juli Baker

PERLA VALTIERRA

San Jerónimo,
Mexico

Some of our favourite homes have come out of the creative hub that is Mexico City, including that of talented ceramicist Perla Valtierra. With a love of exploring new techniques, crafts and cultures, Perla has spent over fifteen years honing her craft, drawing inspiration from her extensive travels and studies in Paris, Kyoto and Brussels. Perla is a true aesthete with an unwavering vision to create pieces that are made to last a lifetime.

San Jerónimo is a residential neighbourhood far from the hustle and bustle of popular Condesa Roma. The secluded area holds a special place in Perla's heart. 'I love that my place is tucked away in a quieter neighbourhood. In twenty minutes by car, I can be in the national park, which feels a world away from the city. The national university campus is also close by and I enjoy spending time walking around it on weekends.'

Perla recalls the serendipitous timing of moving in just before the Covid-19 pandemic. 'I feel very lucky to live in this house. It's an oasis in the city and feels like a hideaway from the busyness of everyday life. It's also situated next to the only open river in the city. When I'm at home, it feels like I'm on holiday, which is such a nice sensation for life in a big city.'

Perla's bedroom is one of her favourite spaces, thanks to the abundance of natural light and the view of Mexico City, not to mention the mountains beyond. 'I love the way that the light changes in my room during the day,' she says. 'It's just a lovely, cosy place to hang out.' Her enchanting bedroom is a simply styled escape kept intentionally minimal to enhance the industrial fittings and geometric ceiling, which stretches right through the house.

The living areas of Perla's home are filled with a curated collection of art and objects, some made by her, some sentimental creations passed down through the generations. Among them are photographs from her father, some of her most precious pieces, which help to infuse her living space with a sense of nostalgia and familial warmth.

It's no surprise that Perla's unique clay works are scattered throughout her abode, with hand-thrown vases and tableware offering both beauty and function. Her creative practice began at university, where she discovered ceramics as part of her industrial design course. A win at a ceramics lab competition ignited her passion for the art form. 'For a long time, I made ceramics simply because it's what I loved doing, with no desire to start a business,' Perla says of her design journey. 'I started creating commercial editions around 2008. I spent a decade in Europe and a year living in Japan, so it's been a lot of learning abroad. I love discovering other cultures and meeting like-minded people. Since being back in Mexico, it's been great to be able to fully focus on my work here.'

Her latest body of work, Xalli, is a collection of glass vessels designed for Nouvel Glass Company. It's an ode to her heritage and a tribute to ancient Egyptian techniques. 'The word Xalli means sand in Náhuatl,' Perla explains. She details the process of sand casting, a method used in ancient Egypt to deposit and blow glass in moulds marked in sand. The unique pieces stay true to Perla's dedication to delivering both form and function to the home, and they promise to stand the test of time as quality objects designed for the sensibilities of everyday use.

San Jerónimo, Mexico

Perla Valtierra

San Jerónimo, Mexico

'I feel very lucky to live in
this house. It's an oasis
in the city and feels like a
hideaway from the busyness
of everyday life ... When I'm
at home, it feels like I'm on
holiday, which is such a nice
sensation for life in a big city.'

Perla Valtierra

San Jerónimo, Mexico

Perla Valtierra

San Jerónimo, Mexico

RYAN JAMES CARUTHERS

& JON ANTHONY

Echo Park,
United States

The beautifully curated home of photographer Ryan James Caruthers and designer Jon Anthony is a unique Spanish-style apartment that sits atop a hill in Echo Park, Los Angeles. The space is both an inspiration and a sanctuary for the couple's shared love of art, rare objects and design. Ryan and Jon speak about the intuitive and rewarding process of infusing new life into the apartment and share stories behind their most cherished vintage finds.

'The space holds a lot of charm and character, which is what drew us in when we were looking for our next home,' Ryan says. 'The building has a very unusual castle-like ambiance, with some incredible views of the city. The rooms feature vaulted ceilings with ornate linework, curious wooden built-ins and white plaster walls decorated with original Spanish gothic sconces and motifs. We had originally intended to replace the fixtures to better fit our aesthetic, but we eventually learned to lean in. Our goal has always been to retain the natural charm of the space while opening up a new dialogue with our curated additions.'

The couple furnished their bedroom with minimalist intent, focusing on creating a tranquil space dedicated to rest. As Ryan explains, 'Our bedroom is styled minimally to create a space solely designed for sleep. On the right side of the bed, a wooden fish sculpture by Korean artist Minjae Kim is encased by a found ornamental carved frame. Beneath the sculpture is a crown-shaped elm chair attributed to Olavi Hänninen. There is also a vintage Akari-style lamp resting on top of an octagonal arts and crafts-style side table on the other side.'

Ryan and Jon's appreciation for objects that hold emotional resonance and have lived multiple lives is evident throughout their home. They continuously collect pieces that tell stories, and gravitate towards items with a rich history. 'We tend to shift items from room to room as we acquire new pieces, finding the place where they fit our space best at that specific moment in time,' says Ryan.

'One of our favourite pieces is a large-scale painting we found buried behind stacks of chairs in a vintage store,' adds Jon. 'It's a sketch of the Battle of Hastings, done in 1935 by Italian artist Pasquale Giovanni Napolitano. We had originally intended to place it in our bedroom, but, when we brought it inside, we realised it would fit better in the living room due to its size.' Another favourite piece in the couple's home is a handcrafted bent-aluminium-and-walnut bookstand designed by UK-based artist Louie Isaaman-Jones. 'The bookstand utilises vintage Roman loom weights on string cords to weigh down the pages of a book,' Ryan says. 'Our collection of art books has completely overflowed from the built-ins onto stacks on the floor throughout the rooms of our home. We will most likely eventually drown in them.'

Ryan draws inspiration for his creative practice from various genres, including portraiture, landscape and fashion photography. He sees photography as a method of visual communication and aims for his projects to feel distinct and palpable. 'I've always seen myself as somewhat of a collector, so I have become quite encyclopaedic when it comes to photographs and visual references,' he says. 'I find myself returning to the same themes while creating – identity, queerness and human emotion. I've recently been exploring my relationship with the environment and how that is reflected in the images I make.'

Echo Park, United States

70

Ryan James Caruthers & Jon Anthony

In addition to furniture and art, Ryan and Jon are also avid appreciators of craft, with an ever-growing selection of ceramic work dotted around their home. 'Our collection is mostly from Japanese artists and potters,' says Ryan. 'A specific favourite is an eighteenth-century Kurawankazara plate - Japan's first version of to-go plateware created with the rise of food stalls. It was apparently common for people to throw these takeaway ceramic plates into rivers, where they were then found over a hundred years later.'

Jon, formally trained in architectural design, explores various art disciplines, including interiors, ceramics and set design. He finds his rhythm with a variety of short-term projects and long-term architectural endeavours. 'There is something nice about the mix between working on short-term projects versus the longevity of an architectural project,' he explains. 'At Studio Shamshiri, I've been working on a lot of kitchens, which prompted us to take a closer look at our own apartment's kitchen - a room that didn't hold the same weight as the rest of the home.'

72

'Our goal has always been
to retain the natural charm
of the space while opening
up a new dialogue with
our curated additions.'

Ryan James Caruthers & Jon Anthony

VALERIE NORMAN

Annandale,
Australia

In the vibrant suburb of Annandale in Sydney's inner west, Valerie Norman, the accomplished men's image director at Kult Models, has crafted a home that embodies her unique and finely honed sense of style. Alongside her husband, Ben, and their beloved borzoi dog, Odessa, Valerie has transformed the house into a space filled with warmth and creativity.

'We found it three days before it went to auction and knew right away this was the place for us,' Valerie shares. The home, a former corner store dating back to 1898 with the original facade intact, underwent a renovation in 1996 by architects who used it as both their living space and office. 'Despite that being over twenty years ago, it still feels very contemporary,' says Valerie. 'It's not for everyone, but we love it.'

The living room stands as the central hub of the home, exuding comfort and flooded with natural light. Valerie describes it as her favourite spot, where she can unwind, listen to music and spend quality time with Odessa. 'It's super comfy with a big couch and lots of natural light.'

Valerie and Ben's bedroom feels neutral and minimal in its aesthetic. Valerie explains, 'I like a bedroom to have just the necessities: the bed with fresh linen, an artwork we love above the bed, a chair, mirror, chest of drawers - minimal clutter.' Looking out onto an internal Zen garden, complete with Japanese maple, their bedroom is imagined as a tranquil retreat to relax and unwind.

Art plays a significant part in Valerie and Ben's home, with their collection curated over the more than nine years they've been together. 'Most works have been made by our talented friends,' Valerie explains, including artists such as Thomas Jeppe, Emile Zile, Anna Pogossova, Misha Hollenbach, Catherine Flora Murray, Bobby Virgona and Komfy. 'These works are special to us because they are all so different and are all by people we really love.' A duo of pieces by Thomas Jeppe fringe the stairwell. They are a joyful addition to the couple's abode that reflects their fondness for punchy art and eagerness to put their individual stamp on their space.

At the rear of the property, Valerie and Ben's home extends to a lush garden and veggie patch that the couple enjoys tending to. 'Having the veggie patch during lockdown was really handy and inspired me to cook much more!' Valerie laughs.

Music holds a special place in Valerie's heart, and she has enjoyed exploring it both as a DJ and in her personal life. 'Some of my best memories have definitely been made DJing with friends at their parties, at bars, clubs and fashion events,' she reminisces. At home, her eclectic record collection takes pride of place in the dining room. It includes everything from John Carroll Kirby to Tom Misch and Yussef Dayes, with cherished favourites such as Solange's *A Seat at the Table* and Alice Coltrane's *Journey in Satchidananda* always making their way back into her playlists.

Completing their home is beautiful Odessa, a cherished member of the family. 'We got Odessa around the same time we moved into our house,' Valerie explains. 'She's a real character and we love her quirks! She's always making us laugh.'

With its unique blend of history and contemporary architecture, and the presence of much-loved Odessa, Valerie and Ben's home exudes warmth, creativity and a genuine sense of belonging.

Annandale, Australia

Valerie Norman

Annandale, Australia

'Our artworks are special
to us because they are
all so different and are all
by people we really love.'

Annandale, Australia

CATH & JEREMY BROWN

Devon,
United Kingdom

The home of Cath and Jeremy Brown is an enchanting farmhouse that could easily have been pulled from the pages of a fairytale. The property, nestled amid the bucolic charm of rural Devon, is the product of the couple's decision to embrace a slower pace of life with their young family.

'We live in rural Devon in an old longhouse – parts of it are five-hundred-plus years old,' Cath explains. 'There are no straight lines, every door is a different height, and not always regular human height, and in some places the walls are half a metre thick.'

Deciding to embark on a tree change, Cath and Jeremy left behind the bustling hubbub of central Hackney, London. 'We moved down here for a slower pace of life and some headspace. We spent some time experimenting with a pottery wheel that we'd bought on impulse from a potter on the moor – it was just before Christmas and we had both our families coming to stay, but not enough plates and bowls, so we made them! And a table big enough for everyone to sit around – it's still our kitchen table – and then we just enjoyed it so much we carried on designing and making, experimenting with different materials.'

The Browns have leaned into the whimsical quality of the property. 'We're currently building a tree house in the garden,' says Cath. 'It's got charred larch sides and overlooks a field where the deer graze at dawn, so the idea is that if you sleep over in it, you'll have a perfect view with your morning cup of tea.' It's an enchanting two-floor design, crowned with a lantern and adorned with a home-dug-clay sink – a true labour of love.

The couple's discerning eye extends to the objects with which they surround themselves. 'We trawl through antique shops finding really simple, basic things that are just so elegantly thought out,' Cath says. 'When we moved here, a friend gave us a Victorian silver egg-coddler that was designed to enable people to boil their eggs at the table. It works perfectly still, if you can find eggs small enough to fit inside, and is just a beautiful object. Aside from old finds, though, our first thought when we need something is to design and make it.'

Beyond artistic pursuits, the Browns nurture a commitment to sustainability and ethical living, inspired by the beauty that surrounds them. 'Being environmentally aware is second nature round here,' says Cath. 'We're surrounded by wilderness, or as close to it as you can find in England at least, so we're conscious of leaving it be as much as possible. We have our own borehole for water, we grow much of our own veg – although I'm currently in an ongoing battle with some hungry rabbits. We shop locally as much as possible and eat very little meat – only that reared by people we know!'

'We're currently building a tree house in the garden. It's got charred larch sides and overlooks a field where the deer graze at dawn, so the idea is that if you sleep over in it, you'll have a perfect view with your morning cup of tea.'

Devon, United Kingdom

87

88   Cath & Jeremy Brown

As their handmade homewares business, Feldspar, grew, the Browns found themselves in need of a dedicated creative studio. 'We've set up a studio on a cider farm about twenty minutes away in some old Victorian barns,' Cath says. Their daily sojourn through hills and fields offers sweeping views of the rolling moorlands and an ethereal mist during autumn. Feldspar's essence is formed through the use of local resources. Cath explains, 'Our china clay comes from Cornwall and is made up into bone china slip in Stoke-on-Trent.'

The Browns' resourcefulness extends to the garden, where they unearth, process and craft their own unique clay – it has a deep orange-red hue that complements the pristine white of fine bone china.

Cath and Jeremy's ever-growing creative practice includes lamps and lampshades. 'Bone china lends itself so well to light,' Cath says. 'It can be cast so fine as to glow like a lantern when lit from within, but then is white opaque otherwise … We're also currently exploring how to hold scent in underfired china and experimenting with creating one hundred per cent natural scent diffusers using only underfired bone china.'

Cath & Jeremy Brown

Cath & Jeremy Brown

INGRID RICHARDS

& ADRIAN SPENCE

Bowen Hills,
Australia

La Scala is a shining example of the melding of personal taste and professional ethos that occurs when architects design their own homes. With a portfolio of retail, hospitality and civic projects under their belts, Ingrid Richards and Adrian Spence, founders of architectural practice Richards & Spence, have drawn on a wealth of experience and an array of influences to create a truly unique home.

The design and construction of the house was an organic process, responding to the site's unique topography and surrounding urban environment. 'When we acquired the site, there was a single detached timber house at the front, which had been substantially altered with little of the original fabric remaining,' Ingrid explains. The elevated courtyard, wrapped in a protective embrace, offered a private sanctuary away from the bustle of the city streets. 'The topography was key to establishing a private courtyard protected from the street.'

This thoughtfully designed courtyard became the heart of the home, centred on a pool that maintains visibility through an inverted fence, creating a unique dialogue with the outdoors.

Ingrid and Adrian's design-led approach is evident in every aspect of La Scala, including their serene bedroom. 'Originally conceived as two bedrooms, the main bedroom occupies the entire lower level and the full width of the southern elevation,' Ingrid says. 'A double-height wall of glass to the south is a cinema of skyscapes, particularly when summer storms roll in.' The generous space allows for versatile furnishings and a rotating, eclectic art collection that ranges from Michael Zavros's mesmerising photorealism to Sally Gabori's landscape abstractions. A work by iconic Australian photographer Bill Henson finds company with an anonymous portrait discovered in the streets of Marrakech.

Ingrid and Adrian's home is a treasure trove of souvenirs from their travels and curated art and objects. 'We travel frequently and widely. Our home holds the souvenirs of our travels together and a collection of furniture and lighting designed by our favourite architects,' Ingrid reveals. Among the cherished items is a large ceramic vase that miraculously survived its journey from Amsterdam in hand luggage. A clamshell from the original home serves as a nostalgic reminder of the property's metamorphosis.

Ingrid and Adrian consider themselves custodians of their built environment in a symbiotic partnership, constantly striving to be part of the city's evolution rather than a static endpoint. Each project, regardless of scale, serves as a prototype for the next, a perpetual exploration of possibilities and an ever-evolving contribution to Brisbane's vibrant landscape.

Ingrid Richards & Adrian Spence

Bowen Hills, Australia

Ingrid Richards & Adrian Spence

'We travel frequently and widely. Our home holds the souvenirs of our travels together and a collection of furniture and lighting designed by our favourite architects.'

Bowen Hills, Australia

Ingrid Richards & Adrian Spence

Ingrid Richards & Adrian Spence

Bowen Hills, Australia

Ingrid Richards & Adrian Spence

JESSICA KRAUS

San Clemente,
United States

Jessica Kraus and her husband, Mike, found their dreamy 1960s San Clemente ranch home just a mile from the Pacific Ocean, and renovated it to encompass a vibe of coastal ease.

The family's design journey began when they acquired the ranch house, recognising its hidden potential despite its unassuming facade. 'We bought it last year knowing it needed lots of work, but it was one of the only houses we could afford in the area, and we were desperate to settle our family here,' Jessica explains.

The renovation process proved to be both an exhilarating experience and a test of resilience. 'We were sort of naive in the beginning,' Jessica admits. 'As we went on, the plans grew more and more involved and, before we knew it, we were gutting the entire house to switch up the main layout.'

Living through the renovation with four kids challenged Jessica in unforeseen ways. 'It felt a lot like camping,' she quips, recalling the makeshift living arrangements, occasional water and electricity disruptions, and the feeling of living in constant disarray. 'But it's also been fun and exciting to see the work pay off and our vision come to life in creating a little sanctuary by the beach.'

Amid the chaos, Jessica found design inspiration in the quiet tranquillity of the houses of Hydra, Greece. 'I love how they lean on all-white interiors with rustic wood accents, imperfect plaster and white-beamed ceilings,' she says. 'I love the simplicity and old-world charm they embrace so beautifully in their beach homes over there. I've long been obsessed with Leonard Cohen's house in Hydra, so I kept coming back to those images when making certain design choices, hoping to secure a small part of that charm.'

Jessica's home is filled with objects of meaning that breathe life into the space, such as the small plaster handprints her boys made in kindergarten. When thinking about the complexities of raising her kids, Jessica says, 'The biggest challenge is how much they seek, crave and feed off risk, in any shape or form. Except for my second son, Leon. He avoids it at all costs. Caution is his middle name. The other three, though, they're constantly throwing themselves off rocks or scaling hillsides and launching off makeshift skate ramps and all kinds of other wild and worrisome things.'

Living close to nature in San Clemente holds a special meaning for the Kraus family. The small-town feel and rugged shore resonate deeply with their love for coastal living. 'Living by the sea feels invigorating in so many ways. Almost like it becomes part of your DNA, which I love. The local longboard community has become a big part of my boys' lives and we love that they feel a part of something so special, and are out in the water as much as possible,' Jessica says. 'Lying outstretched in the sun when the stress of renovation gets to be too much has been my one saving grace through this whole process.'

The disruption has been worth the reward, and Jessica is looking forward to embracing a series of simple joys - cooking in her charming new kitchen, savouring moments with her boys, writing and running along the beach.

'I love how they lean on all-white interiors with rustic wood accents, imperfect plaster and white-beamed ceilings [in Greece]. I love the simplicity and old-world charm they embrace so beautifully in their beach homes over there.'

110   Jessica Kraus

San Clemente, United States

Jessica Kraus

San Clemente, United States

'I've long been obsessed with Leonard Cohen's house in Hydra, so I kept coming back to those images when making certain design choices, hoping to secure a small part of that charm.'

Jessica Kraus

San Clemente, United States

BRAHMAN
PERERA

West Melbourne,
Australia

In the world of Australian interior design, Brahman Perera is renowned for his ability to craft spaces that exude warmth, personality and a deep sense of sanctuary. He shares his beautifully restored home in West Melbourne with his partner, Jason, and their two miniature poodles, Billie and Ella. The house is a seamless blend of heritage charm and contemporary design.

Built in 1865 in the heart of early Melbourne, the house carries an important history as a residence for some of the city's first workers. Reflecting on a 2020 renovation project, Brahman shares, 'We aimed to shape the house in a delicate and respectful way, introducing order, clarity and light to the space. Our goal was to maintain the charm of the original house while adapting it to our new way of working and living.

'We love a house that you physically interact with, where you can shape the architectural settings on a daily basis. The ability to open or close vintage concertina oak doors, adjust curtains and connect the terraces provides movement and theatre, and adds to our own pleasure of living in the house.'

The couple's approach to furnishing revolves around creating a space that reflects their lifestyle. 'Our house isn't merely a showpiece for the entertainment of others,' Brahman explains. 'It is designed to enhance our own enjoyment and pursuits. Each element is intentionally chosen to suit who we are and how we live.'

The master bedroom stands as a testament to these thoughtful design choices. 'To bring intimacy to this large space, we painted the room a deep verdant green and introduced oversized lighting that both creates drama and fills the space. Lying on the bed, I love the interplay between the soft fabric moon-shaped pendant and the billowing crisp white linen curtains. The entire room comes alive with movement and energy.'

Brahman's work as an interior designer is marked by a profound understanding of the balance between sentimentality and intent, beauty and functionality. His creative journey has been shaped by a wealth of experiences in architecture, interior design and fashion.

'I strive to create extraordinary experiences out of the ordinary. My goal is to infuse spaces with emotion and purpose, transforming them into sanctuaries that resonate with the unique stories of those who inhabit them.'

West Melbourne, Australia

120   Brahman Perera

Brahman's manifesto encapsulates his approach to design. 'What we expect of design should be no different from food: complete nourishment for the body and mind.' This guiding light underscores his belief in the transformative power of design, which has the capacity to provide comfort, protection, inspiration and upliftment. Through his work, Brahman endeavours to create spaces that offer holistic nourishment and fulfilment, reminding us all to invest in our surroundings as a form of self-care.

Brahman's design philosophy also draws heavily from his multicultural upbringing, where he observed the power of sentimentality in shaping one's connection to a space. 'I was raised in a diverse, migrant household combining Hindu and Catholic faiths, so an important part of my upbringing was listening to my family share stories and memories of Sri Lanka. I came to understand the religious iconography and antiques in our home as touchstones for my parents to recall memories,' he explains. 'Honouring personal narratives is at the heart of my design approach. I seek to incorporate cherished pieces that hold deep meaning for my clients. I often choose handcrafted, artisanal items because their provenance is personalised and authentic. The story of an object made by one set of hands and cherished by another is incredibly heartening.'

Brahman Perera

West Melbourne, Australia

'I strive to create
extraordinary experiences
out of the ordinary.
My goal is to infuse spaces
with emotion and purpose,
transforming them into
sanctuaries that resonate
with the unique stories
of those who inhabit them.'

124   Brahman Perera

Brahman Perera

West Melbourne, Australia

ANA HOP

Lomas Altas,
Mexico

Nestled in the lush outskirts of Lomas Altas, Mexico City, is a sanctuary that quietly blends an idyllic mix of architecture and nature. Home to photographer Ana Hop and her partner, Sebastian, this unique property is a labour of love that has come together over more than a decade.

'Sebastian has called this place home for around fifteen years, meticulously remodelling and reconstructing over half of the house,' Ana says. 'We have been living together here for just over three years now.'

The dreamy location strikes a balance between countryside living and urban convenience. 'The best part of this area is the sensation of living in the countryside,' Ana explains. 'It's a relatively central area close to many interesting Mexico City neighbourhoods. We're very close to the edge of Chapultepec Park, which we think is the nicest and most expansive green area in the city.'

The real magic of the residence lies in its dialogue with the nature surrounding it. Ana expresses her deep appreciation, saying, 'One of the things I love most about this place is being surrounded by green. We have a lush garden and grow lots of our own fruit and vegetables.' Amid the serenity, which is only occasionally interrupted by visits from hummingbirds, their home becomes an escape from the colourful and sometimes chaotic atmosphere that characterises many parts of Mexico City.

Ana and Sebastian's bedroom carries a sense of calm. 'We love how spacious our bedroom is. It has a terrace with beautiful views to the east so the sunrise each morning is always uplifting,' Ana says. 'This also applies to the bathroom, where we have an outdoor bathtub and shower on a small patio filled with plants. At certain times of the year, we can eat figs from the tree while we shower. We love that it has the feeling of a suite with areas to sit and read or ponder, or spend a lazy Sunday morning enjoying life.'

All the objects in the home carry personal stories. 'We have carefully picked every object in the house, from beautiful natural objects to furniture and artwork. Some we made ourselves, others are from friends and family, and the rest have been acquired with care and patience,' Ana explains. 'We have also been building the library, although at the moment its content is quite motley!'

Ana's passion for photography was kindled by time spent tinkering with her mother's camera and nurtured through her studies in communications and photography in London. Reflecting on her artistic endeavours, Ana shares, 'My creative process always comes back to the story that I want to tell. It involves thinking very honestly about a theme or subject and looking past how photogenic something might be to focus on the bigger picture.'

The couple's thoughtful and patient approach to design has created a retreat that feels immediately laid-back and lived in, in the best possible way.

'One of the things I love most about this place is being surrounded by green. We have a lush garden and grow lots of our own fruit and vegetables.'

Ana Hop

134   Ana Hop

'We have carefully picked
every object in the house,
from beautiful natural
objects to furniture and
artwork. Some we made
ourselves, others are from
friends and family, and
the rest have been acquired
with care and patience.'

PIP & NIC
APLIN

Trafalgar South,
Australia

Hidden away in the wild landscapes of Gippsland is the beautiful home of Pip and Nic Aplin. Affectionately named 'The Nak', a nod to its previous incarnation as a knackery, the property is a source of great pride for the creative couple and their two charismatic Bengal cats, Ernest Hemingway and Margot Tenenbaum. Pip loves unique design pieces, the hunt for an artwork that will become the soul of the home, and quiet weekends among the trees.

The abandoned building underwent a metamorphosis, blending contemporary design with the echoes of its former life. Set on three acres at the edge of the Uralla Nature Reserve, Pip and Nic's only neighbours are myriad creatures of the Australian wilderness.

Pip and Nic, who previously lived in a city warehouse apartment, relish the peace and quiet now afforded to them. 'Waking up to a view of treetops every morning is never a bad way to start a day. Having moved here from the city, the peace and quiet is very much appreciated and savoured,' Pip muses.

The couple's bedroom is clad in dark plywood with oversized windows framing the trees beyond, creating a seamless merging of inside and out. Clever design places the wardrobe downstairs next to the bathroom, creating space for custom room-length bookshelves that house Pip's collection of novels. A plush armchair by CCSS perfectly complements the room's dark tones and beckons readers (and feline friends) to indulge in peaceful moments of respite. The pièce de résistance is a Louise Hearman painting, its dark wooden frame and blue-green hues blending seamlessly with the surrounding view. 'If there can be a most favourite thing of all the favourite things in this room, it has to be my Louise Hearman painting that hangs quietly on the wall adjacent to the bed,' Pip says. 'When you take a moment to study the image you realise, as with all Hearman paintings, that there is actually a little more going on than scenery. It is just magic.'

Art and objects of deep significance can be found in every corner of Pip and Nic's home. 'We have a painting downstairs that I found while trawling art gallery online stockrooms in one of the many lockdowns in 2021. I was searching for a piece that would speak to and for this house and after many, many hours of hunting, I came across this amazing painting by Lottie Consalvo. It's called "It held the sky above the sea" and there could simply not be a more perfect painting for this space,' Pip enthuses. Straddling the stairs between the dining and lounge spaces, the artwork is a rich focal point for the open-plan living area.

The couple's love for furniture and design is present throughout their home, as each carefully selected piece contributes to a truly immersive and considered space. 'We are both very much visual people and are inspired and driven by beauty, by form and by craftsmanship,' Pip explains. 'I, especially, am a through-and-through furniture groupie, and have an obsession with finding standout pieces that combine to create an experience and bring us joy. Nic, as an artist, is very inspired by our surroundings and the idea of contrasting the natural and built human worlds. The Nak is the ultimate realisation of this combination.'

While the allure of their home often keeps them within its tranquil embrace, Pip and Nic also enjoy their surroundings. 'On weekends, we actually spend the majority of our time here at the property!' Pip laughs. 'I work in the city during the week, so to have a couple of uninterrupted days to exist as a little family in our own private forest is, more often than not, too good to pass up!'

'Waking up to a view of treetops every morning is never a bad way to start a day. Having moved here from the city, the peace and quiet is very much appreciated and savoured.'

Pip & Nic Aplin

'We are both very much visual
people and are inspired and
driven by beauty, by form
and by craftsmanship.'

Pip & Nic Aplin

Pip & Nic Aplin

Trafalgar South, Australia

NEADA
DETERS

Echo Park,
United States

The idea that less is more seems to be a recurring theme when you speak to Neada Deters, founder of the organic skincare range LESSE. It's a philosophy that underpins the development of her products, which have been described by *Vogue* as being concerned with 'quality not quantity': each ingredient in the range is precisely selected to be transformational, and to work in harmony with the others. This same principle extends to Neada's beautifully renovated mid-century home, where she and her husband, Drew, recently settled in Echo Park. With a view of treetops, the property exudes a feeling of light and openness, accentuated by a thoughtfully curated collection of vintage furniture and art.

'Our previous home was just the next suburb over, but we really love the community in Echo Park,' Neada explains. 'So many of our neighbours have lived here for decades and there is wonderful proximity to nature. Our street borders one of the largest parks in Los Angeles and our local hiking trail is just a few feet from our front door.'

The couple's home was converted a decade ago by a previous owner, who was a prolific collector of art. Neada shares, 'The space is really a gallery designed for living. The bones are mid-century – one of my favourite architectural periods – and internally it has been opened up to allow an immense amount of natural light to flood through. My favourite feature, though, is the large tree that our deck was built around. It provides a beautiful canopy of natural shade.'

In the bedroom, Neada embraces her love of minimalism and objects of meaning. She says, 'I'm naturally a minimalist but, where I do fill space, I usually gravitate towards vintage furniture and objects either created by friends or collected on travels.' The most notable piece of furniture in the room is an exquisitely crafted bed. 'Our bedroom really centres on our bed, which was handmade in the US. Our bedside tables are vintage Milo Baughman burl wood, and they're quite wide and tall so our dog sleeps under one of them. On each side table, we usually stack all the books on our reading lists alongside vases by my dear friend Rachel Saunders.'

Art and objects play a significant role in Neada and Drew's home. Reflecting on their collection, Neada shares, 'Almost all of our furniture is vintage and it's difficult to choose between them, but I am thrilled about our recent purchase of vintage black leather and chrome dining chairs by Mies van der Rohe – one of my favourite designers and architects. I also love my recent art purchase, a watercolour on canvas by British-born but New York-based artist Joe Henry Baker. I hope to collect a few more of his pieces in the future.'

Neada's home strikes a clear balance: it's far from sparse, but thoughtfully curated, intentionally dressed. As Neada describes, the decoration of her abode has been a process, one that intentionally hasn't been rushed, but has naturally evolved over time. 'As someone who has moved across continents, I find myself reflecting often on what home means to me. It is, simply, a space of comfort and calm. I find that with my family and friends, and here in the openness of each room. There was never an intention of approaching this space with a minimalist lens but we always wanted to take it slow, and evolve our home through the deliberate addition of each enduring piece. Almost all of our furniture is vintage or handmade for us, so each one is added with great intention.'

'I'm naturally a minimalist
but, where I do fill space,
I usually gravitate towards
vintage furniture and objects
either created by friends or
collected on travels.'

Echo Park, United States

Neada Deters

Echo Park, United States

156   Neada Deters

Echo Park, United States

Neada Deters

159

STEPHANIE STAMATIS

Brunswick West,
Australia

Stephanie Stamatis welcomed us into her lovingly renovated 1960s apartment in Brunswick West. A talented stylist, Stephanie lives with her husband, Timothy, and their adorable baby girl, Saška, along with their feline companion, Bunny. 'What I love most about our home is the light and the space,' Stephanie shares. 'The proportions and windows are generous, in a special way that older apartments can offer. The building is set on top of a hill and our views open out over the valley so we can watch the weather.'

As you step into the family's sunny living room, it's immediately clear that Stephanie and Timothy have cultivated an environment that radiates individuality. Stephanie has purposely conjured an oasis of warmth, creativity and personal expression. A multitude of art pieces and cherished objects fill the space, reflecting her eclectic style. 'I often joke that my home looks like the "before" shot on a *Hoarders* episode.' Stephanie laughs. 'There are countless little things I'm attached to - souvenirs collected from my travels. They hold precious memories for me and a connection to the places I've been and the experiences I've had. Silly Italian candies and *David* souvenirs, a breadstamp from Macedonia, ceramics from Japan and even a 1980s Cy Twombly poster from Paris. I especially love my Bode Senior Cord cushion; it's absurd and beautiful with hand-drawn smiley faces and nasturtiums.

'In my dining space there is a handmade arts and crafts-style chair with these beautiful faceted legs and one of my newest finds, a French still-life painting of peaches in a silver bowl. But if there was a fire, I would grab the photos of my grandmother and our parents when they were kids.'

The master bedroom is enveloped by a sense of serenity and tranquillity - a sanctuary within the colourful home. 'Our bedroom is a cocoon,' Stephanie describes. 'It's nice for sleeping when it's raining outside and hanging out in bed with the baby and cat. It's the kind of room that asks for simplicity as a remedy to all the layering happening in the living areas.' But it's not a space devoid of personality - angular lighting and decorative mementos bring both warmth and interest to the bedroom.

Stephanie's passion for her craft is evident throughout the home. 'I don't have a studio at the moment so my living room turns into a shooting space,' Stephanie explains. 'The dining area, with its built-in seat, doubles as my workspace. It is all connected to the kitchen, so I can watch a pot of beans on the stove while I work. I like working on this smaller scale for now.'

Stephanie's career as an art director and stylist has been a journey of self-discovery and evolution. From her early days of colouring within the lines as a child - 'I started my design career as an emo art-room kid in high school and then drawing glitter names on Christmas baubles at shopping centres' - to her forays into interior design and the freelance world, she has honed her craft and discovered her true passion lies at the intersection of food and still-life.

'I am a true homebody, and my love language is nurturing through food, so heaven for me is being at home with Tim, Saška, family and friends, eating around our dining table.'

Brunswick West, Australia

Stephanie Stamatis

Stephanie's creative process is a careful balance between imagination and practicality. She explains, 'Before embarking on a project, I like to spend some time brainstorming to see if it is something I feel I am able to take on in the first place. I have tried to be a little more selective with how I spend my work time; being a new mum I actually haven't had a choice. I then delve into discussions with clients, gathering essential information - dreams, desires and objectives. From there, I dive into a world of references, curating ideas from my own collection of images, books and memories.' This amalgamation of inspiration and vision is distilled into an art-direction document - a roadmap that brings Stephanie's client briefs to life. 'It's a fun puzzle, piecing together the perfect location, lighting, sets and props - from there I call the team in and produce the shoot!'

Outside of her professional endeavours, Stephanie finds immense joy in creating a nurturing and inviting environment at home. 'I am a true homebody, and my love language is nurturing through food,' she says, 'so heaven for me is being at home with Tim, Saška, family and friends, eating around our dining table.'

Stephanie Stamatis

'There are countless little
things I'm attached to …
They hold precious
memories for me and a
connection to the places
I've been and the
experiences I've had.'

Stephanie Stamatis

Stephanie Stamatis

TARA
MAYER

& SEBASTIAN
PRANGE

Vancouver,
Canada

Historians, writers and adventurers Tara Mayer and Sebastian Prange epitomise the essence of a life well travelled. Their journey has led them across continents and through diverse cultures. Now they have settled in their idyllic home in the mountains of Vancouver, a true sanctuary brimming with warmth and character.

'We met doing PhDs in Indian history at the School of Oriental and African Studies in London,' Tara recalls. 'Sebastian was a few years ahead of me, and we were soon close friends. Our story isn't simple but, reflecting back on it, it had a life force of its own. In Emily Dickinson's words, "The heart wants what it wants – or else it does not care."'

Though they had different upbringings – Tara in Hawaii and Sebastian in Germany – they share a sense of being global citizens. 'We each left home quite young, Tara to an international school in Britain and me to travel around the world,' Sebastian explains. 'Tara was in Paris for a long time and I haven't lived in Germany since my teens. My elder daughter was born in London, my younger in Vancouver. Which is to say, at this point, I think we relate rather little to our national identities. Perhaps that's what makes living in a country as defined by immigration as Canada so appealing to us.'

Travel has played a pivotal role in shaping the couple's worldview, instilling in them an insatiable curiosity for the world and its cultures. 'My dad had lived and worked in Nepal before settling in Hawaii, and my mother is from India,' Tara shares. 'Growing up on Maui, we spent most summers with family in Kerala or backpacking through Asia. In my late teens and twenties, I travelled mainly in Europe and the Nordic countries as well as in North Africa, capturing scenes in watercolour and through photography. I've always been fascinated by weaving and textile traditions as well as food culture and pottery. For me, travel is synonymous with education – with personal, creative and intellectual growth.'

Sebastian's early years in Europe laid the foundation for his love of exploration, leading to a solo journey around the world. 'I spent two years bumming around, house-sitting in Laurel Canyon, working in coffee shops and developing film,' Sebastian reminisces. 'Some of my greatest travels have been related to my research – the deserts of Yemen, the port cities of South India.'

175

Tara Mayer & Sebastian Prange

Tara shares the story of their home. 'After so many years in huge cities, we yearned for nature, and Vancouver is a rare city in which wilderness exists so close to downtown. We fell in love with a post-and-beam house from the late 1950s and did a gentle renovation with David and Susan Scott, very gifted architects who've since become friends. There's a large reservoir at the end of our road that looks like a fjord, a ski resort just up the hill, and forest trails everywhere. We love cultivating our garden, cooking, lighting fires and falling asleep to the sound of rain. Gaston Bachelard's words resonate deeply: "The house shelters day-dreaming, the house protects the dreamer, the house allows one to dream in peace."'

It was the house's simplicity that initially attracted the couple's attention. 'Our home was built in 1957. It's a simple post-and-beam house, using local fir and cedar,' says Tara. 'It's a very modest but true expression of the design principles and values of its time. What captured us most, though, was the discreet scale and openness of the house, and its south-facing windows. They allow the secluded and mature garden to feel almost like an ever-changing extension of the interior.'

For Sebastian, the open-plan nature of the home perfectly provides everything their family needs. 'Our home consists of just two open levels, with the kitchen and living space downstairs and bedrooms above. Our downstairs living space shelters all our waking hours. It's where we read, talk, work, cook, eat, unwind and play.'

The couple's mornings begin with gentle family moments, as Sebastian brings Tara tea in bed, savouring the calm before their youngest daughter stirs. Their daily journey to the university where they work takes them through the scenic beauty of Stanley Park and along the mesmerising English Bay.

In contrast, evenings at their home come alive with the laughter of their children and stories shared around the table. 'There's usually loud music and a lot of dancing after dinner.' Tara laughs. 'Then, Sebastian tidies up while I bathe our daughter. We snuggle into bed, where I tell her stories in the dark or listen to her ramble about her day (and, currently, her dreams of being a dog owner) until she nods off. I often fall asleep beside her but sometimes I sneak out of bed for a film with Sebastian, or quiet conversation or just a glass of wine and work emails.'

Although they've settled into their home, their thirst for exploration still thrives. Tara and Sebastian frequently travel for research and conferences, visiting Paris, London and India. 'Stockholm, Kyoto and the Faroe Islands top our current list of places to visit, but we'll take our time,' Sebastian muses. They're also eager to explore more of Canada after a road trip through Banff and Jasper left them in awe.

Tara Mayer & Sebastian Prange

'After so many years in huge
cities, we yearned for nature,
and Vancouver is a rare
city in which wilderness
exists so close to downtown.'

Tara Mayer & Sebastian Prange

CAMILLE LADDAWAN MOIR

& ZACHARY FRANKEL

Collingwood,
Australia

This century-old house, home to Camille Laddawan Moir, her partner, Roslyn, and their friends Zachary and Anna, was lovingly designed and renovated by Camille's family and has a gentle, lived-in feel. The group have cultivated a warm and inviting space that serves as both a peaceful retreat and an inspiring hub for their respective creative practices.

Camille fondly recalls the rich history of the property. 'The house used to belong to my uncle, auntie and cousin, who lived here for fifteen years before they moved to Dja Dja Wurrung country. I love that it has their heights marked and written in the door jamb, that the sounds in the house are soft, as everything is so worn-in, that the kitchen floor dips like a small hill and the back of the house is glass so we can see the garden in full. I also like that my uncle planted a gum tree when he moved in and I also planted one when I moved in.'

Zachary describes the house as a transformative escape. 'Stepping into the house through a hand-carved door off loud and gritty Johnston Street, you are instantly transported. Inside, it's spacious and tranquil. There's a theatricality about the place; it's very dramatic, with almost cathedral-height ceilings, painted walls that have developed a patina over time, an internal Juliet balcony and decorative columns. I feel like I'm part of an elaborate performance every day.'

Both Camille and Zachary take great pride in their bedrooms, which reflect their personalities and artistic sensibilities. Camille and Roslyn's bedroom has two large, arched windows that flood the space with diffused light and offer views of rooftops and the sky. Camille explains, 'My favourite thing about our bedroom is that it feels both connected to the street and goings-on below, as well as a peaceful hideaway. The original floorboards are painted cream and layered with scuffs from years of use, and are now bowing off their nails in sections. Our walls are duck-egg blue, the fireplace is pewter – though it doesn't work – and a big handwoven rug, which was the first thing we found for the house together, hangs on the entry wall.'

Zachary sees his room as a haven for relaxation and creativity. 'My room is cosy and cocoon-like. It's kind of in the middle of the house, on the first floor, so there's no noise from the street. I have one of my mum's paintings on the wall and have just recently added some of my own pieces to the space; a ripple mirror frames your face when you walk into the room, and a crinkle lamp produces beautiful ambient light and creates a feeling of calm.'

186   Camille Laddawan Moir & Zachary Frankel

The home's interior is laden with artworks and curios gifted by friends and family. Camille shares, 'Our home is filled with objects and art that friends and family have made or gifted over the years, so it's hard to choose favourites!' Some specific pieces are a woodblock print by Ella Mittas, which hangs in their kitchen, a ewer by Camille's friend and former housemate Layla Cluer, and a blue-and-white weaving, which reminds Camille of whales.

Zachary finds inspiration in the furniture designed by Camille's uncle, Kim Moir, saying, 'Being surrounded by his work has been really inspiring to me and I'm sure has influenced my own work. This includes the marble-top console table, which was inspired by Émile-Jacques Ruhlmann and was a sixtieth birthday present to Kim's wife, Maria; the floor-to-ceiling bookcases, which give the living room so much space and grandeur; the copper-and-oak kitchen, which transports you straight to France; and the chaise longue, which looks out through floor-to-ceiling glass to the courtyard and a lovely gum tree.'

Living in a creative household proves to be a tremendous asset for everyone. The housemates are collaborative, frequently exchanging ideas, sharing artistic discoveries and falling naturally into discussions that fuel their creative processes. 'We affect each other in many more ways than I think we imagine!' Camille says. 'It's those passing comments, the offhand questions and answers, creative moods, showing each other pictures of things we like, talking about design and what we do each day, that help inform each of our work. It's very special and it's lovely to be around Zac.'

Camille's creative practice began during the early days of the pandemic, offering her a chance to explore the intricate art of beading. 'Beading has given me an avenue to connect my research into philosophical and historical ideas of language and symbolism with aesthetics and the hands-on, technical aspects of art-making,' she explains. 'I'm thankful that I had the opportunity to devote so much time to something I wouldn't have otherwise been able to explore. I've really fallen in love with it.'

Zachary's creative pursuits span an array of disciplines, from furniture design to sculpture and lighting. 'I have a broad range of approaches to my design work,' he says. 'Sometimes playful and explorative, I will make something for the fun of it or experiment with a technique and see what comes of it … Sculpture is different again. I will usually start by making a series of maquettes in plasticine or something similar. I like being able to model something quickly and get a feel for the shape and scale and then find a piece of material to suit it.' He adds, 'I think there are lots of subtle ways that we help each other. It's a lovely relationship that spans creative and personal areas of our lives. Everyone in the house is very encouraging and, when I come home from the workshop feeling dispirited or discouraged, they are often there to pick me up and offer some constructive advice.'

'There's a theatricality about
the place; it's very dramatic,
with almost cathedral-height
ceilings, painted walls that
have developed a patina
over time, an internal Juliet
balcony and decorative
columns. I feel like I'm part
of an elaborate performance
every day.'

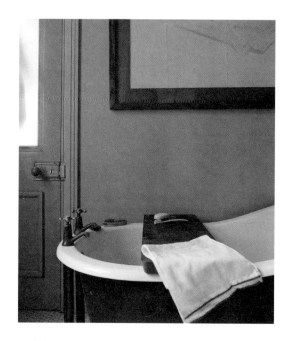

188   Camille Laddawan Moir & Zachary Frankel

Camille Laddawan Moir & Zachary Frankel

Camille Laddawan Moir & Zachary Frankel

LIVIO TOBLER

& POPPY KURAL

Pearl Beach,
Australia

Idyllic Pearl Beach is where furniture designer Livio Tobler, his partner, artist Poppy Kural, and their young daughters, Etta and Delphi, escape the frenetic energy of city life. While the small seaside town is just an hour and a half outside Sydney, it seems a world away thanks to its dramatically slower pace.

The humble beach shack that has become their home away from home may be simply dressed but is rich in a long history of family gatherings and milestone moments - after all, it's belonged to Poppy's family for the past forty-odd years. 'It's one of the original beach houses in Pearl Beach,' says Livio. 'Once a fisherman's cottage, it's now been in the family for thirty-seven years, and hopefully for many more to come.'

Largely untouched, the shack's interiors remain an ode to the past, an intentional acceptance of the house as it is. 'It's an untouched time capsule with all-original interiors. It's really a magical spot being so close to the beach and the surrounding national park,' Livio explains. A sense of familiarity and nostalgia greets you at the door, courtesy of a healthy collection of paintings and drawings adorning walls, and family photographs, many taken by Poppy's grandmother, Mutzi.

Slow days spent swimming or traipsing the nearby national park are what Livio holds dear. Being outdoors was what led him to furniture design in the first place. Initially a graphic designer, Livio quickly realised that the office environment and constant screentime were not conducive to his creative aspirations. Seeking something more hands-on, he decided to explore carpentry and furniture design. Starting with small, experimental projects using found materials, Livio soon discovered his talent and passion for creating functional and thoughtfully crafted furniture, which he sometimes crafts from the Pearl Beach escape.

'I loved designing, but I wasn't cut out for the office environment. I always had an idea of getting into industrial or furniture design,' Livio shares. 'I thought doing a carpentry apprenticeship would allow me to gain knowledge and skills in constructing physical objects and structures.' And, while Livio has worked on various projects throughout his career, he finds particular joy in creating furniture for those closest to him. 'I'd say there are special moments in most projects, but particularly special ones would be making things for friends and family.'

A long-time meeting place for the whole extended family, this home is a destination to gather for celebrations of all shapes and sizes. 'We usually go to Pearl Beach because we are celebrating a birthday or Christmas, or enjoying a family long weekend with cousins. So Etta associates going there with lots of fun and love around,' says Livio.

For Poppy, it's a joyful case of history repeating itself. 'I grew up experiencing Pearl Beach the way my daughters do now,' she says. 'It's pretty special taking our kids there, generations later. Lots of memories have been made there.'

'Up until recently, Etta was an only child,' adds Livio. 'Going to Pearl Beach meant that she had lots of cousins running around with her. The house is located opposite the beach. It's always so special sitting on the deck after dinner, overlooking the ocean and seeing all the kids playing in the sand dunes.'

Pearl Beach, Australia

Livio Tobler & Poppy Kural

'It's an untouched time capsule with all-original interiors. It's really a magical spot being so close to the beach and the surrounding national park.'

Pearl Beach, Australia

200   Livio Tobler & Poppy Kural

Pearl Beach, Australia

201

FERNANDA CABALLERO

Valle de Bravo,
Mexico

The vibrant home and studio of artist, yogi and proud Gemini Fernanda Caballero is set among the greenery of Valle de Bravo. Filled with treasures from travels and many (many!) animal friends, including cats, dogs, turtles, a rescued cockatoo and a ferret named El Buki, the space is a reflection of Fernanda's colourful approach to life and has become a true haven.

'I've lived in this place almost two years now. It doubles as a studio and home,' Fernanda says. She moved into the house just as it was completed in November 2019. Little did she know, her timing would prove to be advantageous, as much of Mexico, and the world, went into lockdown in March 2020. Fernanda reflects on this serendipitous timing. 'The home enveloped me at a time when everything and everyone - including me - was going loco! I felt very fortunate that I got to live and nest in the house I designed. I love that every little space and corner was designed by me, and it all works together as a safe haven. I really put my heart and soul into creating this house. When I am home everything feels at peace, even if it isn't.'

The bedroom holds particular charm for Fernanda. She shares her delight in two unconventional design choices: 'Firstly, the orange carpet, my favourite in the house, which I found in Marrakech and spent two days negotiating on the price; and, secondly, the golden velvet curtains which surround the whole room.' These elements, though initially met with uncertainty, fill the room with a unique aura and ambiance. 'At night, when I close the curtains, I am surrounded by a golden haze, which feels really dreamy,' Fernanda says. 'It's kind of seventies ... a bit adventurous and fun and cosy.'

The home is infused with a treasure trove of personal creations and carefully chosen pieces. The walls feature Fernanda's paintings, creating a mini-gallery of her life. Beyond her own art, she has thoughtfully collected textiles and ceramics from her travels, and they add to the fabric of stories throughout her home.

While art and design are an important part of her life, Fernanda's passion for yoga and wellness has also played a significant role. Her journey into yoga began after a dance injury when she was fifteen. She was initially hesitant, but yoga's magic slowly worked its way into her life, eventually leading her to embrace the practice wholeheartedly. 'I started attending every class I could, understanding what it was really about. Essentially, I became a yoga enthusiast.'

In addition to her artistic and yoga practices, Fernanda runs Veintiséis Taller Textil. The store, located in Mexico City, showcases antiques and textiles from her global travels, each item telling a unique story.

Valle de Bravo, Mexico

206 Fernanda Caballero

Valle de Bravo, Mexico

209

'I love that every little space
and corner was designed by
me, and it all works together
as a safe haven ... When
I am home everything feels
at peace, even if it isn't.'

Fernanda Caballero

Valle de Bravo, Mexico

Fernanda Caballero

Valle de Bravo, Mexico

QIANYI LIM

& ROSS PAXMAN

Forest Lodge,
Australia

Qianyi Lim and Ross Paxman's striking home is in a league of its own. Completed in mid 2020, Stable House began as a dilapidated horse stable on a piece of land alongside regenerating bush. For Ross, design practice founder of Primary Works, and Qianyi, co-founder of architecture practice Sibling, the project was deeply connected to family: new arrivals - the couple welcomed their daughter, Linya, in 2022 - and all the relatives who spend time there.

The innovative build is a successful merging of old and new, inspired by the surrounding landscape. 'Our home sits on Gadigal land, at the rear of an inner-city block in Forest Lodge, Sydney, between tightly packed terraces on one side and a native bushland reserve on the other,' explains Qianyi. The house is built within the remnants of a late-Victorian horse stable. Many of the original brick walls are still clearly visible both inside and outside the house.

It's within arm's reach of Sydney city centre, but this architectural statement feels a world away. 'Being so close to the bush reserve here is quite magical,' says Qianyi. 'There's very little city noise and we hear birds all day long. The house was designed to celebrate the history of the site and the brick walls of the stables, but also to become an extension of the nearby bushland and a place to enjoy it.'

Windows, and plenty of them, encourage natural light in abundance, helping to welcome the outside in - especially when it comes to the creative couple's bedroom. 'Our bedroom is upstairs. It has a framed, full-height window looking out to the reserve next door,' describes Qianyi. 'It feels like we are in the middle of the bush rather than inner-city Sydney.' Her favourite addition to the sleeping space isn't an artwork or family heirloom - it's their new family member. 'Our favourite "thing" in the room right now is probably our baby, Linya! She hasn't quite made the transition to her own room downstairs. In her cot, there is a very special patchwork quilt made by her grandmother thirty years ago.'

Building Stable House was a lesson in patience. The process, including approval, took around six years. 'My most useful skill was probably keeping Qianyi calm in the face of some stressful situations with builders and neighbours!' Ross jokes.

Qianyi reflects on their journey. 'The design was submitted to council all the way back in 2014, so it's been a long process! Since then we've refined quite a lot. Ross also had a bit more input - we had only just got together when the design was first planned out. My sister Xinyi was also involved and may eventually live here one day, so many of the design decisions were made around her work as a chef, with the kitchen being quite large and a central feature of the house.' The industrial-style cooking space, with lengthy (and hard-wearing) stainless-steel benches and ample storage, makes for a kitchen that's both practical and in keeping with the space's distinct aesthetic.

Forest Lodge, Australia

Qianyi Lim & Ross Paxman

The couple clung to the celebration of smaller moments and achievements to maintain enthusiasm along the way. 'Things started to feel real the day they started removing the stable roof and stalls, leaving only the three coarse, thick brick perimeter walls in place. It was the first time we were able to experience their full, uninterrupted height. Another milestone was the concrete pour, and another big day was the crane coming down our narrow street to erect the steel framing for the roof. This really started to define the full volume of the house.'

While the home is remarkable in its own right, there is also a burgeoning art collection decorating the walls. 'We have many artworks and objects made by our friends, including a digitally generated tapestry work by Ry David Bradley and an abstract ceramic piece by Jia Jia Chen, both of which hang in the main living space,' says Qianyi. 'We often burn incense from our friends at Subtle Bodies, and we love our ceramic mushroom incense burners from Komfy, a local artist. We also drink a lot of tea and have several special teapots, including a set by Matteo Thun for Memphis, and a family heirloom pot of Chinese porcelain that lives in an insulating woven cane basket.' Qianyi and Ross gather treasures as thoughtfully as they built the home in which they sit.

'The house was designed
to celebrate the history of
the site and the brick walls
of the stables, but also to
become an extension of
the nearby bushland and
a place to enjoy it.'

Qianyi Lim & Ross Paxman

222

Qianyi Lim & Ross Paxman

EMILY L'AMI

Pasadena,
United States

The home of Emily and Fred L'Ami, founders of artisanal perfume house Bodha, proves that work and leisure can comfortably coexist. The duo's revamped 1950s ranch-style house is tucked away in the hills of Los Angeles, fringed with no shortage of greenery and home to a pack of coyotes. With open spaces, restrained decor and an adjoining work studio, it's a place where the creative couple can dabble in both business and pleasure.

'It's been life-changing,' says Emily of the couple's recent move to carve out a space dedicated to their business. A staid office it is not - the minimalist building neighbours the main house and is immersed in the surrounding garden. 'We wanted to create a place that feels like a sanctuary,' says Emily. 'We focused on ensuring every space looks onto views of green. We've planted one side of the land; next, we'll plant a big scent garden so people can smell the perfume materials from plant to bottle.'

For Emily and Fred, good design is interwoven with a sensory experience. This mentality is evident in their home, and it sits at the heart of the Bodha brand. 'When we're designing something for Bodha, we're thinking about how we want you to feel when you use it,' says Emily. 'Every sensory detail sends a message to your subconscious. We're hoping you can tune into that moment, pause and enjoy.

'We created Bodha to inspire people to live a more sensory life. Of all the senses, scent significantly influences our emotions because it bypasses our thinking mind and goes straight to our subconscious. It's so primal and mysterious and the next frontier in the science of the body-mind connection.'

This is why the smell of Emily and Fred's home is just as important as the furniture and finishes. Their days are suffused with ritual and scent, from morning through eve. 'I love lighting our incense while I make coffee in the morning - coffee and incense is a great scent combo! Before I go to sleep, I use one of our perfume oils. It might seem odd to some people to use perfume before bed, but I see it as sending a message to myself about how I'd like to feel.'

Emily explains, 'Our bedroom is a little oasis. It has windows and French doors which open out onto the garden. My favourite thing is drinking coffee and reading in bed with the garden breeze floating in, especially when there's a chill in the air and I'm warm under the covers.'

A neutral colour palette greets you indoors, with plentiful natural light from the many windows and a very personal collection of artwork. 'Our most precious piece is an artwork that friends and family gave us as a wedding present,' says Emily. 'It's a big close-up photo of a rock by a New Zealand artist, so it's also a reminder of home. We've lived in a few different countries over the years, and that's helped us home in on the pieces we love enough to bring them with us again and again. It's always the things made by people we know or mementos from our travels.'

It's no surprise that Emily and Fred have been so intentional with the dressing of their home, considering their design ethos. 'Good design is a form of care,' says Emily. 'Something made with intentionality resonates differently; it's a form of unspoken communication between the maker and the end user.'

'Good design is a form
of care. Something made
with intentionality resonates
differently; it's a form of
unspoken communication
between the maker and the
end user.'

Emily L'Ami

Emily L'Ami

'I love lighting our incense
while I make coffee in the
morning – coffee and incense
is a great scent combo!
Before I go to sleep, I use one
of our perfume oils.'

Emily L'Ami

About the author

IN BED is a home textiles brand based in Sydney, Australia. Creating timeless, beautiful products in a responsible and respectful way, we aim to inspire our community through meaningful design and by sharing stories to encourage positive change.

Founded in 2013 by Pip Vassett, IN BED is driven by the creative space - the type of home that is so full of warmth and character that you never want to leave.

Find us at INBEDStore.com or @inbedstore.

Credits

TILLY BARBER
Eltham, Australia
Photography: Tasha Tylee, Melbourne
Words: Matthew Lennon

ANNIE NGUYEN
Koreatown, United States
Photography: Annie Nguyen, Los Angeles
Words: Matthew Lennon

MAGGIE DYLAN & JULIAN KELLY
Coorabell, Australia
Photography: Maggie Dylan, Coorabell
Words: Elisha Kennedy

JOHN & JULI BAKER
West Toronto, Canada
Photography: Norr Studio, Toronto
Words: Elisha Kennedy

PERLA VALTIERRA
San Jerónimo, Mexico
Photography: Ana Laframboise, Valle de Bravo
Words: Matthew Lennon

RYAN JAMES CARUTHERS
& JON ANTHONY
Echo Park, United States
Photography: Ryan James Caruthers, Echo Park
Words: Matthew Lennon

VALERIE NORMAN
Annandale, Australia
Photography: Natalia Parsonson, Sydney
Words: Matthew Lennon

CATH & JEREMY BROWN
Devon, United Kingdom
Photography: Beetle Rhind, Devon
Words: Elisha Kennedy

INGRID RICHARDS & ADRIAN SPENCE
Bowen Hills, Australia
Photography: Yaseera Moosa, Melbourne
Words: Matthew Lennon

JESSICA KRAUS
San Clemente, United States
Photography: Elizabeth Carababas, Los Angeles
Words: Elisha Kennedy

BRAHMAN PERERA
West Melbourne, Australia
Photography: Phillip Huynh, Melbourne
Words: Matthew Lennon

ANA HOP
Lomas Altas, Mexico
Photography: Ana Laframboise
& Daniel Klinckwort, Valle de Bravo
Words: Matthew Lennon

PIP & NIC APLIN
Trafalgar South, Australia
Photography: Tasha Tylee, Melbourne
Words: Matthew Lennon

NEADA DETERS
Echo Park, United States
Photography: Hannah Mills, Los Angeles
Words: Matthew Lennon

STEPHANIE STAMATIS
Brunswick West, Australia
Photography: Phillip Huynh, Melbourne
Words: Matthew Lennon

TARA MAYER & SEBASTIAN PRANGE
Vancouver, Canada
Photography: Gillian Stevens, Vancouver
Words: Elisha Kennedy

CAMILLE LADDAWAN MOIR
& ZACHARY FRANKEL
Collingwood, Australia
Photography: Tasha Tylee, Melbourne
Words: Matthew Lennon

LIVIO TOBLER & POPPY KURAL
Pearl Beach, Australia
Photography: Leif Prenzlau, Sydney
Words: Matthew Lennon

FERNANDA CABALLERO
Valle de Bravo, Mexico
Photography: Ana Laframboise, Valle de Bravo
Words: Matthew Lennon

QIANYI LIM & ROSS PAXMAN
Forest Lodge, Australia
Photography: Nic Gossage, Sydney
Words: Sarah Bristow

EMILY L'AMI
Pasadena, United States
Photography: Monroe Alvarez, Los Angeles
Words: Sarah Bristow

CONTRIBUTORS
Matthew Lennon
Elisha Kennedy
Sarah Bristow

Thank you

This book would not have been possible without the support of our community and the incredible pool of talent that contributes to and makes the *IN BED Journal* so special.

Thank you to our publishing team at Hardie Grant, particularly Alice and Antonietta for encouraging and guiding us on how to turn our prolific online blog into a beautiful book! We are so grateful for the opportunity.

A huge thank you to our photographers, not only for your magical eyes and work, but for bringing us amazing homes and people to share on the journal.

Thank you to each and every homeowner and feature from over the years; we feel so lucky to be invited into your home. Thank you for sharing it with us. We are forever grateful and so thrilled to be able to share the beauty of your sanctuary each week.

Thank you to our team at IN BED, past and present. A small but mighty group of people spread across Australia (and the world). You are what makes IN BED tick.

A special thank you to Elisha Kennedy, our very first journal editor, who set this series on a wonderful and meaningful path, and wrote and produced a number of the early pieces in this book.

And lastly a huge thank you to Matthew Lennon, our most recent journal editor, who found and produced most of the features in this book as well as crafting the beautiful words.

We are so lucky to have all of you as part of the IN BED fam.

Published in 2025 by Hardie Grant Books,
an imprint of Hardie Grant Publishing

Hardie Grant Books (Melbourne)
Wurundjeri Country
Level 11, 36 Wellington Street
Collingwood, Victoria 3066

Hardie Grant North America
2912 Telegraph Ave
Berkeley, California 94705

hardiegrant.com/books

Hardie Grant acknowledges the Traditional Owners of the Country
on which we work, the Wurundjeri People of the Kulin Nation and the
Gadigal People of the Eora Nation, and recognises their continuing
connection to the land, waters and culture. We pay our respects to their
Elders past and present.

A catalogue record for this
book is available from the
National Library of Australia

Sanctuary
ISBN 978 1 76145 040 2
ISBN 978 1 76144 336 7 (ebook)

10 9 8 7 6 5 4 3 2 1

Publishers: Alice Hardie-Grant, Tahlia Anderson
Project Editors: Antonietta Melideo, Claire Davis
Editor: Libby Turner
Creative Director: Kristin Thomas
Designer: Claire Orrell
Head of Production: Todd Rechner
Production Controller: Jessica Harvie

Colour reproduction by Splitting Image Colour Studio
Printed in China by Leo Paper Products LTD.

MIX
Paper | Supporting
responsible forestry
FSC® C020056

The paper this book is printed on is from FSC® certified forests and
other sources. FSC® promotes environmentally responsible, socially
beneficial and economically viable management of the world's forests.